PRAYING AND FASTING

And

WHY IT'S IMPORTANT IN OUR EVERYDAY LIVES

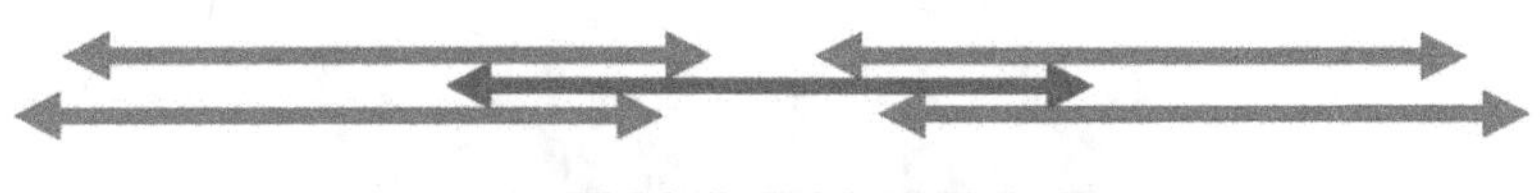

DEISARE TERRY

TABLE OF CONTENTS

WHAT IS PRAYER

I Always Get Asked, "Deisare, How Do You Pray" And My Response always remains the same. It's simple Talk to God Like You Talk to Your best friend. It does not take a lot. You don't have to scream and shout. Speak in tongues, fall out or have this Fancy speech. Be Yourself. God wanna Hear From the Real You, The Broken, Hurt, stressed out, and Down to Your Last You.

So What Is Prayer?

Praying: speaking to God, mainly to express gratitude or to ask for something; communicating with one's creator. In Christianity, fasting and prayer become necessary as one needs to separate the spirit man's needs from those of the physical man.

Food is fed to the physical body to nourish it, but the spiritual man usually receives little, just as Lazarus desired crumbs from the king's table. This is the condition of some Christians' spiritual men, who want to be fed daily through constant communion with God and the place of fasting and prayer.

If prayers are to be said without setbacks like tiredness, time consciousness, fatigue, etc., then the need to fast will be a good decision. In an atmosphere where the spirit man is fed, the physical man, also termed "flesh," loses its grip or hold on the one carrying out the prayer and fasting.

If I'm being sincere, there are times when I enviously think about Eve's lovely experience of conversing with God while on a walk and a discussion. Despite not making the world a better place, Eve undoubtedly changed it. She is the mother of us all!

It so many Great women in the Bible That Had a Prayer life. Like Eve

Sarah, Hagar ,jochebed, Miriam ,Deborah,Rahab ,Naomi,Ruth and

Esther. Hannah

My Favorite one is Hannah. 1 Samuel 1

Listen, Queen, Hannah Prayed So Hard That buddy Thought she was Drunk !!! Yeah, I said, buddy, lol Alright. Let's make it a little more Plan Text For the Super religious Ones lol Sorry, Yall, That Just Aint me; I'm Real, Raw, And Down to Earth!

Hannah Went to the temple; yes, she locked herself in the temple, lay on her face, and sought God for a child. Hannah Prayed so Hard that Eli Thought she was drunk. Can You Imagine wanting something so bad that you cry out to the point you feel drunk? When was the last time you were drunk? You remember that feeling of Everything being a Blur, right? Yeah, that's our Girl Hannah

PRAYER:

Father, The Bible Tells us all Things come through Fasting and Praying. I pray For My Sister in Christ, That's Seeking you for answers and Guidance, God. Please Give her Rest in her mind and give Her Peace in Her Spirit. Lead in Guide her On this Spiritual Journey Amen.

NOTE:

____

____

____

____

____

____

____

____

____

____

____

____

____

____

FASTING?

Fasting is biblical. Growing up in a pentecostal Church, We Fast A Lot !! Typically the beginning of the year, we are called to go on a 21-day fast. There are Many Types of Fast, but the most popular one is the Daniel Fast. Daniel went on a Fast, only eating Fruits and Vegetables for 21 days. Yes, 21 Days !!! 2,000 years ago, fasting was a primary means of humbling ourselves before God. Scriptures mention a common practice called fasting. It involves giving up eating entirely and voluntarily for a fixed period of days, and its aim is to devote oneself to prayer and seeking God.

Whenever a fast is not accompanied by prayers, it then signifies another thing, like fulfilling all righteousness because one is compelled to do it as a result of the religious sect in whom one finds himself or herself; another could be that,

MARY, JESUS' MOTHER: I wish that the prayers of Mary, the mother of Jesus, were better documented among all the biblical ladies of worship. Like Come Mother Mary Was Something Special. As Christ grew in wisdom and knowledge, Mary is known to have transmitted her Faith to him. The angel said, "God liked Mary," Mary Had Crazy Faith. We know this relates to a relationship in which she constantly and vulnerably prayed. Luke records one prayer for our benefit during his gospel.

PRAYER:

❖   Thank you for starting today's significant journey with me. Thank you for erasing fear from my hand and helping me prepare for any challenge that lies ahead in Jesus' Name. Amen.

❖

❖ Father, as I begin my fast today, I ask for Your blessing to help me truly experience and understand the importance of my fast and how, just like the disciples, I can use this time to renew my Faith and sharpen my focus once more.

❖ Thank you for the gift of fasting and for allowing me to join you on this journey, knowing there will be many benefits. Amen.

NOTE:

____

____

____

____

____

____

____

____

____

____

TERMS OF FASTING AND PRAYER

Like Everything else in life, fasting and prayer have rules and restrictions. Fasting is a conscious act; it's a time when a believer goes above and beyond to fulfill his needs and seek his creator's requirements. The disciples of Jesus were asked to heal a man's crazy Kid. Still, they could not do so because of their lack of Faith and neglect of fasting and prayer, which would have created an environment conducive to Faith rising and connecting with God's divine healing power.

Complete Separation

According to **Nehemiah 9:1-2**, fasting is a complete withdrawal from all food, weight, people, and other things for the duration of the practice. Yes, Queen, we gotta stop scrolling on the Gram and opening up that Bible!

Every burden of sin is removed during a fast, which leaves one feeling physically light and able to connect spiritually with ease.

Hebrews 11:11

Can we Talk About SARAH?

Interestingly, Sara is the next praying woman named in Scripture. We don't know Noah's wife or the other ancestors, but we assume they prayed, Right? Why? Because their children learned how to pray, primarily passed down through mothers? Let me tell you, I grew up in a household where my mother used to walk the floors Rebuking the Devil, speaking in Tounges, and screaming Glory, Glory, glory !!! On a 3 way call carrying olive oil, anointing every person in the house, I fully understand how Sarah's kids turned into prayer warriors.

However, Sarah is remembered as a person of great Faith, and even though Genesis does not contain a prayer, one can see from Hebrews that she possessed tremendous confidence. Without prayer, a person of Faith cannot arrive; Sarah was one of many praying women in the Bible.

Let us Tap into our Faith Like our Sister Sarah!

PRAYER:

Lord, please forgive me for craving food more than you. Forgive me for craving anything more than you. Lord, redirect my hunger. Be my God. The Bible Tells us that if we have Faith as small as a mustard seed, we can say to a mountain move. Increase My Faith. Help me to trust you even more and increase my Faith like Sarah Amen.

NOTE:

____

____

____

____

____

____

____

____

____

RESPONDING TO GOD'S CALL

Fasting and prayer become mandatory for every child of God. Before embarking on any God-related assignment, he/she must subject himself/herself to fasting and prayer as done by our Lord Jesus before He began his ministry here on earth, as recorded by Matthew in the fourth chapter of his book.

Fasting and prayer are a season of preparation for one's God-given purpose. It gives the believer an advantage over physical things, first due to being subdued and then spiritually, through worship of the Almighty.

Genesis 16:13 is a Good Read. Check it out !!

Okay, let me just say this because we sometimes get confused when we take this walk seriously and surrender our lives to God. Everything is going to be peaches and cream! Nope, that's when all hell gonna break loose but trust me, You gonna be okay. Don't give up. God gotcha queen

Let us go a little deeper and talk about

HAGAR. What captivates me about our God is that He is not racist, sexist, or any other "its." He loved the people of Israel. That much is unavoidable, but He loved all the Colors in the world Our Heavenly Father created. Look at The Beautiful Story and LifeLife of Hagar.

Sarah and Abram did not treat her with honor or dignity, but God did. God noticed her, spoke with her, he gave her a reward. Her plea was very potent, and we can see the first name given to God—the God who sees!

PRAYER:

Father God, Fasting is a Sacrifice, And It Takes Strenght; God, I Asked that you give my Sister in christ strength to make it through her Fast, Beat down Her flesh, and Remove Every Distraction That Might come to hinder her today. God give her Grace. Help her to get into your Presence Even More. As she Humbled Herself before you, seeking you never like before, I pray that she is led by you, Father, in not the world. In Jesus' Name. Amen

NOTE:

TIME WAITING FOR A RESPONSE

Anna lived to see the birth of Jesus, as told by God, and stayed in the place of fasting and prayer until the fulfillment of the promise of her seeing the Messiah before she died.

In **Acts 13:2**, it is recorded that the Holy Spirit spoke to the church to separate Paul and Barnabas for their missionary journey to the

Gentiles. In the place of fasting and prayer, answers to questions and pending issues are found.

Let us not forget Hannah prayed, "My heart exults in the Lord, and my horn is exalted in the Lord. My mouth speaks boldly against my enemies. Because I rejoice in Your salvation." 1 Samuel 2:1

HANNAH, you knew I was gonna spin the block on my Girl Hannah! I told you she was my favorite, lol.

Whenever you discover a faithful man in the Bible, I hazard to assume that he had a praying mother, but Hannah stands out above the rest. The priesthood's path was transformed by her noble sacrifice and prayer in sending Samuel to the temple to be raised as a priest.

God used Hannah's Son Samuel in powerful ways through preaching, prophesy, and admonition. This Kid Had a calling on his LifeLife from his Mother's Prayers and sacrifice. All of this began with the prayers of a desperate mother. How Many times have we been Desperate Queens? Hannah is one of the Bible's many praying women. It and Also My Favorite, As I said before.

Okay, I know you wondering why she keeps spending so much time on Hannah or Boosting her up when she said its so many great women in the Bible. Okay, so listen, I was once like Hannah. I was 17 years old, and my son was dying at two. I locked myself in the bathroom, begging God to please send me a child because I still have no other reason to be here if my firstborn son has transitioned on. Queen, I felt so desperate like Hannah, and God gave me my daughter, so Hannah is lowkey my best friend in my head, lol.

PRAYER:

Lord, I want Your word to penetrate my heart so profoundly that it becomes my word! I want to see things in your eyes, hear something in your ears, and feel things in your feelings. I want to line up with you so that my hearts beat in syncopation together in Jesus' Name. Amen.

NOTE:

____

____

____

____

____

____

____

AN EXIT FROM TROUBLE

When one has nothing to do during a day of hardships and is fasting, one can still practice fasting. The soul can then readily connect with our God to get Guidance. When Daniel was sent into the lions' lair, King Darius could not sleep. **Dan 6:18**

Daniel used the fasting and prayer season to seek God about God's word in redeeming the Jews from Babylon after the time limit had passed.

And Naomi said to her two daughters-in-law, "Go, return each of you to her mother's house." "May the Lord deal kindly with you as you have dealt kindly with the dead and me." "May the Lord grant you to find rest, each in

her husband's house?" Then she kissed them, and they lifted their voices and wept." Ruth 1:8-9 NIV

Honey Ruth was stuck with her mother-in-law. And we all know how these mothers-in-law can be, but you know I'm not even gonna touch that, lol Thank God for Good mothers inlaws.

NAOMI:

Let us go ahead and talk about Naomi, a biblical woman I can relate to and sympathize with. Life was hard for her as her husband made tough choices that took her away from Everything she knew to a more complicated life. She returned to Israel after being widowed and bereaved by the deaths of her children.

Losing a child is a pain you will never get over. So yes, I sympathize with our Sister Naomi!

Why didn't she just stay and turn to the gods of Moab? Because Naomi was a devout person who adored and trusted God, it follows that she prayed. Ruth also joined the family for Christ as a result of their faithfulness! Talk about making the world better!

PRAYER:

Lord, I praise You that once Your Word becomes deeply ingrained in my heart, my spoken words will unleash rivers of strength and authority against the devil's plans to destroy me! I am grateful that, just as Your words created the cosmos, my spoken words of Faith alter my environment! In the Lord Jesus, I offer my request. Amen

NOTE:

____

____

____

____

____

____

____

____

____

____

____

____

____

____

____

IMPORTANCE OF FASTING AND PRAYERS

Fasting and prayer are necessary for Christians to ultimately seek the Face of God.

Greater Closeness to God

By denying our carnal nature, we can satisfy God's demands. We can discover what He desires for our lives through prayer and fasting. Due to fasting, our spirit and soul feel delighted. It's a choice to temporarily put our flesh to death to accomplish the higher purposes of a tremendous God looking for us. Mark 2:20.

"Now before they lay down, she (Rahab) came up to them on the roof and said to the men, "I know that the Lord has given you the land, and that the terror of you has fallen on us, and that all the inhabitants of the land have melted away before you." "For we had heard how the Lord dried up the water of the Red Sea before you when you came out of Egypt." Joshua 2:8-10 NIV

Our Good Sister RAHAB:

Rahab's story is another one that makes me feel emotion. A woman from another nation changed the world with Faith in God. As a result of her dedication, the spies' lives were saved, and her family ultimately changed the course of history. In Matthew 1:5, she is identified as the mother of Boaz, establishing a link between her and David and, ultimately, Jesus. How can I be sure that Rahab was among the numerous Bible women who prayed? A righteous person, Boaz. God spared only Rahab's family when she witnessed Jerico collapse all around her. Your Faith grows more substantial when you see God, and you may pass that on to your kids.

"However, Rahab the harlot and her father's household and all she had, Joshua spared; and she has lived in Israel to this day, for she hid the messengers Joshua sent to spy out Jericho." Joshua 6:25 NIV woman in a white robe praying in a field

Can we take the time and think about a time you found yourself going through hell, And God brought you out on top? Like you watched your child or sibling go through something that should've destroyed them, but God gave them Grace! Yes, aint he good? Let us Pray

PRAYER:

Heavenly Father, as I grow weary, I am strengthened by knowing that my fasting journey is about much more than just the nourishment I put on my plate. My focus returns as you remind me of the significance and importance of fasting, which draws me closer to you. It is essential for me to remain focused now, during this time, and to avoid distractions that could cause me to stray from the spiritual path that I am on. Thank you, Lord, for a sacred way that I know will bear spiritual fruit. Amen.

NOTE:

____

____

____

____

FASTING and praying SERVE MULTIPLE PURPOSES

We live in a Trying Time, so we need To seek God Daily. Before I start my day, I allow myself 20 mins to lay awake, simply talking to God to help me to begin and control my day. We need help, Guidance, and wisdom, .sometimes even just to make it through the Hecked day. The Moment I Go on A fast All Hell Break Lose. Listen, Queen, when I Tell You Everything that could go wrong, go wrong, honey, it does!! But God Gives us Grace and mercy to get through. Like the things sent to destroy you don't even touch you! It might happen, but you will get the victory outta the attack. Attacks come to build up your Spiritual Man, Your Character. If you didn't Experience it, How can You share it to encourage the next? God offers us help by asking us to pray and fast. The verses I mentioned below Help you understand what praying and fasting make possible for Christians:

❖ Praising Our Heavenly Father *(Nehemiah 9);* granting courage *My Good Sister (Esther 4:16)*
❖ Loving your enemies, *Girl I know this is hard to do, but it is something God instructs us to do ..(Psalm 35:12-14);*

reconciling yourself or your country to God *(Daniel 9; Nehemiah 9)*;

❖ God's promises *(Luke 2:36–38)*; wisdom *(Acts 14:23)*

Prayer is essential, and fasting is a must. Still, the discipline of using Praying and Fasting together can help us make LifeLife in a world Like today more bearable by linking us to God and Pulling on His power instead of our own.

Then Esther told them to reply to Mordecai, "Go, assemble all the Jews found in Susa, and fast for me; do not eat or drink for three days, night or day." I and my maidens will also fast in the same way. "And thus I will go to the king, which is not according to the law; and if I perish, I perish." Esther 4:15-16

Pick that Bible up, and Fact check me, Queen!

Let us talk about ESTHER:

In the Life of Esther, we see prayer and fasting. This was a woman positioned by God to change the world powerfully. Because of her loyalty, devotion, and courage, the entire race was spared a holocaust. It wasn't the first time, nor would it be the last time someone tried to wipe Israel off the face of the planet, but God intervened through this praying woman and her influence!

Esther is Like Our Praying Grandmother, who sits in her chair praying God covers her whole legacy, Praying Generation Curse off her Grandchildren and their children; listen because of Esther, the entire race was spared! We still getting by with our grandmother's prayer.

Come on, Queen, Let US pray!

PRAYER:

Father, cleanse my heart so I can focus on You and You alone as I Give my thoughts, worries, disappointment, and hurts to You. God, help me with this Depression, Anxiety, loneliness, infidelity, miscarriage, Rape, abuse, Heartbreak, and fear. Helped me to look for only Your approval and not anybody else; if I have any Sin in my heart, Forgive me, make me over again .help me see anything in my life that is not like you made it so I can turn that part of my life back to You. In Jesus's mighty name amen

NOTE:

____

____

____

____

____

____

____

____

____

____

____

____

____

OUR HEART BECOMES OPEN TO SPIRITUAL REVIVAL

We kindle the Holy Spirit's fire during fasting and prayer; we become change agents and intercessors for the broken and hurting during the period of fasting and prayer as we become sensitive in the realm of the spirit. Hence we connect to the needs of others. Our hearts are revived and refreshed spiritually because of fasting and prayer, as recorded in *Acts 1:8.*

Every believer should cultivate the habit of fasting and prayer to seek the Face of God in total humility and turn aside Everything that keeps them busy.

Fasting and prayer could be corporate, but the personal one becomes essential since it is intentional and self-imposed.

We become all we are intended to be when we follow in the footsteps of Our heavenly Father, our Lord Jesus, through fasting and prayer.

"And there was a prophetess, Anna, the daughter of Phanuel, of the tribe of Asher. She never left the temple, serving night and day with fasting and prayers. At that very moment, she came up and began giving thanks to God and continued to speak of Him to all those who were looking for redemption". Luke 2:36–38

Let's learn about our Sister ANNA THE PROPHETESS:

It is very rare to see women listed as serving in the temple, but Anna the Prophetess is one. She devoted her life to serving God. Prayer and fasting were disciplines she practiced. God blessed her prayer life and allowed her to bless His One and Only Son.

That's Deep, Sis God allowed her to Bless His One and Only Son! Anna's Life was so Straight that God trusted her with his son; wow. Let us Pray

PRAYER:

Lord Jesus strengthens us against the devil's temptations, removes from us all lust and every unrighteousness, and shields us against our foes, seen and unseen. Teach us to do your will so we may love you first and foremost. You are our maker and our redeemer, our help, our comfort, our Everything, and our hope; Thampraise and glory be to you now and forever. Amen

NOTE:

____

____

____

____

____

____

____

____

____

____

____

____

____

____

____

____

____

____

____

____

____

____

____

____

____

____

____

____

____

____

PRAYER HAS INFLUENCE

The Honest Truth about prayer and fasting may make us want to do it more or as often as we can, but here's the catch: Praying and Fasting only work if you're in service of God and not your ego or pride.

Jesus broke it down to us about those who pray and fast for selfish reasons in the Sermon on the Mount:

But not like the hypocrite when we pray; they love to put on a show while standing in synagogues and on street corners(I'm all for going out to get souls, don't get me wrong)so that everyone might see them. They have earned their full reward. But when you pray, enter your chamber, shut the door, (i know yall saw War Room?) If you did not have the opportunity to watch that movie, I highly suggest you do so) Get In Your secret Closet, wash your face, get in your prayer Postures, and address your prayers to your heavenly Father. Then you'll receive a reward from your Father, who knows all your deeds in *Matthew 6:5.*

It's great that you want to pray and fast, but ask God to check your motives before you do. If you're going to pray and fast to feel like a better Christian, stop there and ask God to purify your intentions. But if you're approaching these practices with love and respect for God, you are free to close the altar and do so.

"Then Jesus said to her, "O woman, your faith is great; it shall be done for you as you wish." "And her daughter was healed at once." Matthew 15:28

THE CANAANITE WOMAN:

Matthew tells of an exciting woman who spoke face-to-face with Jesus. The Canaanite Woman isn't even given a name, but her story is given a place in the Bible. She had Faith enough to beg for the mercy of God for her daughter.

"And a Canaanite woman from that region came out and began to cry out, saying, "Have mercy on me, Lord, Son of David; my daughter is cruelly demon-possessed." *Matthew 15:22*

We can assume that after witnessing God's Son's miraculous love, her Faith grew, and became more devoted to prayer. If you have ever experienced God moving in your children's lives, you know there becomes a deep desire to see it again.

That is how I know this is one of the many praying women of the Bible.

PRAYER:

Almighty Father, give me the Grace to know the importance of fasting and prayer in my Christian Life in Jesus's name. Amen.

NOTE:

____

____

____

Father God, I pray for my Sister that she can humble herself in your Presence to break every chain that has been Holding her bound for days, weeks, and maybe years, The hurt she has been holding on to since she was a little girl, That let down she experience when she believes he was going to show up. That broken heart destroyed her trust, self-worth, and dignity, and That Miscarriage made her think she was not good enough, God showed my Sister that she was beautiful and wonderfully made. God brings out that anointing that's hidden deep down inside of her. Restore my Sister, and Make Her Over Again. in Jesus's name amen

Deisare Terry